TEN GREAT
AMERICAN
COMPOSERS

The *Collective Biographies* Series

Collective Biographies

TEN GREAT AMERICAN COMPOSERS

Carmen Bredeson
and Ralph Thibodeau

Enslow Publishers, Inc.

40 Industrial Road   PO Box 38
Box 398   Aldershot
Berkeley Heights, NJ 07922   Hants GU12 6BP
USA   UK

http://www.enslow.com

Library of Congress Cataloging-in-Publication Data
Bredeson, Carmen.
   Ten Great American composers/Carmen Bredeson and Ralph Thibodeau
       p.cm. – (Collective biographies)
    Includes bibliographical references, videography, list of Web sites, and index.
    ISBN 0-7660-1832-6
    Composers—United States—Biography—Juvenile literature. [1.
Composers.] I. Title: 10 great American composers. II. Thibodeau,
Ralph. III. Title. IV. Series.
ML3929.B73 2002
780'.92'273—dc21

                        2001004205

Printed in the United States of America

10 9 8 7 6 5 4 3 2

To Our Readers:
We have done our best to make sure all Internet addresses in this book were active and appropriate when we went to press. However, the author and the publisher have no control over and assume no liability for the material available on those Internet sites or on other Web sites they may link to. Any comments or suggestions can be sent by e-mail to comments@enslow.com or to the address on the back cover.

Contents

Preface

The artists featured in this book do not use paint and canvas to draw their pictures. Instead, they create wondrous images of sound using notes and rhythm. They all seem to have been born with music in their souls. Each one of them began playing a musical instrument while still very young. As they added years and formal training to their lives, their talents exploded.

Just as American people are not of one race or religion, American music is not influenced by just one sound. It is a melting pot of many sounds. We can hear a hint of the great European composers, the beat of the Caribbean, and the tempos of Mexico in our national repertoire.

These ten American composers wrote everything from marches to symphonies, ragtime to grand opera, jazz to string quartets. While it is helpful to read about the composers and their works, the only way to learn about their music is to hear it.

Some of the tunes, like the marches of John Philip Sousa, will sound very familiar to you. It will be hard not to stand up and march while listening to Sousa's music. Other more serious works, like the symphonies of Charles Ives or the sonatas of Samuel Barber, are less well known. They may not make you want to tap your feet, but perhaps you will hear melodies in them that appeal to you.

All of the works discussed in these pages are currently available on CDs or cassette tapes. Why not try listening to a few selections and broaden your appreciation of what American composers have produced? You probably won't like all of it. By listening to selections for each composer, though, you will have a better understanding of the scope and variety of American music. Happy listening.

John Philip Sousa

1

John Philip Sousa
(1854–1932)

Thirteen-year-old John Philip Sousa was going to run away and join the circus to play in the band. The circus performers were leaving town the following night and he planned to be with them. He would have to be very quiet because his parents would never agree to let him go. John had to let somebody in on his grand secret, though, so he ran next door to tell his friend, Edward Accardi. Unfortunately for John, Ed could not keep a secret and John's father soon knew all about the circus plans.

Early the next morning, while John was still in bed, his father came into his room and said, "When you get dressed to-day, put on your Sunday clothes."[1] It wasn't Sunday, but John did as he was told and put on his good clothes. Then he went downstairs and had breakfast with his father. After breakfast, Mr. Sousa said, "We'll take a walk."[2] They walked to the Marine barracks and went into the commandant's office.

On June 9, 1868, John Antonio Sousa enlisted his thirteen-year-old son in the Marine Corps as a boy musician in the U.S. Marine Band. Mr. Sousa had played the trombone in the band since 1850. He and the commandant had discussed John's plans to run away with the circus and decided the Marine Band was a good place for him to be. His father's decision was a good one, because John would later become one of the greatest band leaders in America.

John Philip Sousa was born in Washington, D.C., on November 6, 1854, to John Antonio and Elizabeth Trinkhaus Sousa. His father had come to America from Spain and his mother was originally from Germany. When John was still very young, his father taught him to play the violin. After he started school, John took music lessons in the neighborhood. He often went along with his father to Marine Band concerts. By the age of ten he was sitting in with the band, playing the triangle and cymbals. At the age of thirteen, after trying to run away with the circus, John became an official member of the Marine Band.

John Philip Sousa stayed with the Marine Band until he was nineteen years old. After being discharged from the Marines, Sousa played with several orchestras, including one at Ford's Opera House, where President Abraham Lincoln had been assassinated ten years before. It was at Ford's that Sousa got a big break. One night the regular conductor got sick, and Sousa was asked to take up the baton. Sousa did a great job conducting and was offered a job as leader of a band in Chicago. He became a very skilled band leader and his talent quickly took him from Chicago to New York City.

After arriving in New York, it didn't take John long to fall in love with Jane van Middlesworth Bellis, or Jennie as he called her. She was a member of the chorus in the musical *H.M.S. Pinafore,* and Sousa was conducting the orchestra. They married on December 30, 1879, when Jennie was seventeen years old and John twenty-five. Soon after their marriage, John Philip Sousa was called back to Washington by the commandant of the Marine Corps and asked to be the conductor of the Marine Band. He agreed and moved to Washington with Jennie.

Members of the band were unhappy because of low pay and long hours of rehearsals and performances. Many of the members asked to be discharged from the Marine Band, and Sousa had only thirty-three musicians left by the end of his first year as conductor. He worked hard to improve conditions and gradually built the band up to the full seventy members. The Marine Band played at many official functions in the White House and the Capitol, in addition to marching in parades and giving band concerts.

Before long, Sousa and his band were getting compliments and attracting large audiences. He stayed with the band for twelve years and then left to form his own touring band.

On September 28, 1892, the Sousa Band played its first concert in Plainfield, New Jersey. They then went on an eight-week tour of cities and towns in New England. The band did not become nationally famous, however, until the following year when it was asked to play at the Chicago World's Fair. Thousands of people came to hear the band and went away humming and whistling snatches of songs like the "Washington Post March," which Sousa composed. During all of the years Sousa had been touring, he had also been composing music whenever he got the chance. Among his compositions, he had written several marches.

What exactly is a march? Most people know one when they hear one because it makes them want to get up and MARCH. Actually, it is just about the oldest music we know of. History is full of wars and men marching into battle, accompanied by tunes played on horns, pipes, and drums. Since people have two feet, and marching means putting one in front of the other, marches are written so that the beat is basically one-two, one-two. Marches are not used just for wars, though. They are wonderful for parades and sporting events and band concerts. Marches get people moving.

Largely because of the popularity of Sousa and other bands, soon most towns in America had bands of their own. At the same time, school bands were formed to play at sporting and other events. In no time, there were bands all over America and many of them were playing marches written by John Philip Sousa, who was often called the "March King."

Sousa composed his most famous march on board a ship in 1896, while he and his wife were returning from a European tour. In his autobiography, *Marching Along*, Sousa wrote, "As the vessel steamed out of the harbor I was pacing the deck . . . . Suddenly, I began to sense the rhythmic beat of a band playing within my brain. It kept on ceaselessly, playing, playing, playing. Throughout the whole tense voyage, that imaginary band continued to unfold the same themes . . . . I did not transfer a note of that music to paper while I was on the steamer, but when we reached shore, I set down the measures that my brain-band had been playing for me, and not a note of it has ever been changed."[3]

The march that John Philip Sousa's "brain-band" composed on that voyage was "The Stars and Stripes Forever." After writing the piece down on paper, Sousa took the march to his publisher, who wanted to shorten the name to "Stars and Stripes." Sousa said NO! "I don't mean 'Stars and Stripes,'" he said. "I mean 'Stars and Stripes Forever.'"[4] In 1987, more than ninety years after it was written, "The Stars and Stripes Forever" was declared the official national

John Philip Sousa composed some of the most famous marches in American history including "The Stars and Stripes Forever," which was declared the official march of the U.S. in 1987.

march by the U.S. Congress. What would the Fourth of July be without fireworks, hot dogs, and "The Stars and Stripes Forever"?

From the first time Sousa's band played the piece on May 14, 1897, the march was included in every concert after that. Sousa expert, Paul Bierley, said, "He would have been tarred and feathered and run out of town if he didn't play it. When the March King came to town, you had to hear 'The Stars and Stripes Forever.'" Mike Ressler, librarian for the Marine Band, added, "It gets people standing on their feet, tapping their toes. And if they have a flag in their hands, they're certainly going to be waving it."[5]

"The Stars and Stripes Forever" was just one of John Philip Sousa's compositions. He wrote 136 marches, including "Hands Across the Sea" and "The High School Cadets." He also wrote seventy songs and fifteen works for the stage, beginning with *El Capitán* in 1885. *El Capitán* was the first successful Broadway operetta written by an American. In addition to his music, Sousa wrote three novels, including *The Fifth String,* an autobiography called *Marching Along,* and more than one hundred magazine articles.

John Philip Sousa composed much of his music in his head. Paul Bierley wrote, "He composed without the aid of a musical instrument. He just wrote on paper what he heard in his head. He always carried music paper. If he got an idea, he would write it down and develop it later when he had more time."[6]

The musicians who played in Sousa's band were very fond of their director. "His musicians, believe me, would have followed him to the end of the earth. He treated them with such great respect. He never raised his voice in a rehearsal. If anyone made a mistake, he didn't say anything about it except, 'Let's go over it again,'" said Bierley.[7]

During his long career, Sousa conducted thousands of concerts in America and Europe. People never got tired of hearing his wonderful marches. In his book, *Marching Along*, Sousa wrote, "But inevitably there will come a time when I shall be too feeble to serve my public any longer. When that time comes I shall lay down my baton and say, 'God bless all of you—every member of a faithful following. The love shown me is returned a hundredfold, I assure you, and I am proud to say it. I thank you, every one, for what you have done to make my life so rich in happy memories.'"[8]

On March 6, 1932, John Philip Sousa conducted for the last time in Reading, Pennsylvania. The last piece the band played was "The Stars and Stripes Forever." After the concert, Sousa returned to the Abraham Lincoln Hotel in Reading and died later that day at the age of seventy-seven. John Philip Sousa, the March King, was buried with full military honors in Congressional Cemetery in Washington, D.C.

2

Scott Joplin
(1868–1917)

The town was Sedalia, Missouri, a place most people had never heard of. The location was the Maple Leaf Club, a popular dance hall for African Americans. In 1899, a young musician sat down at the piano and played a piece he had just written, called the "Maple Leaf Rag." That night a star was born. The pianist was Scott Joplin.

Joplin was born near Texarkana, Texas, on November 24, 1868, to Jiles and Florence Joplin. The Civil War had ended just three years before Scott's birth. Jiles, who was a freed slave, worked for the railroad. Florence, who had been born free, did washing, ironing, and housecleaning for other people in the area.

Scott Joplin

"The Joplins were a musical family: Florence played the banjo and sang, and Jiles played the violin. Jiles apparently taught his children the violin as well," wrote Joplin expert Edward Berlin.[1] In addition to the violin, Scott also wanted to learn to play the piano. His mother managed to save enough money to buy a second-hand piano for her son in about 1881. By this time, Florence Joplin was raising her six children alone. Jiles had left the family and was living elsewhere.

Scott took piano lessons from a teacher in the neighborhood and formed a singing group with his brother and two other boys when he was sixteen. The quartet performed at dances and social events. Zenobia Campbell, a Texarkana resident during Joplin's time, said, "He did not have to play anybody else's music. He made up his own, and it was beautiful; he just got his music out of the air."[2] Scott also played the piano in local clubs, but he dreamed of wider horizons. At the age of seventeen, he left Texarkana and made his way up the Mississippi River to St. Louis, Missouri.

St. Louis was an important center of both classical and popular music at that time. Scott Joplin found work playing the piano in nightclubs around St. Louis. His music attracted many fans and soon he was playing in towns all over the Midwest. While in St. Louis, Joplin continued to study music with conductor Alfred Ernst. In 1901, Ernst said of his student, "With proper cultivation, his talent will develop into positive genius."³

Joplin got tired of moving from place to place and decided to settle in Sedalia, Missouri, located about two hundred miles west of St. Louis. Sedalia had become a gathering place for music lovers. In addition, Smith College was located in Sedalia, and Scott Joplin wanted to go to school and study music.

In 1904, Joplin moved to Sedalia, and soon found work playing the piano in the Maple Leaf Club. The type of music Joplin played was called *ragtime*, which introduced a new kind of foot-tapping rhythm into popular music. Ragtime caught on because it was fun to listen and dance to. Many of Sedalia's most important residents visited the Maple Leaf Club to hear Scott Joplin play. His "Maple Leaf Rag" quickly became a favorite with his fans.

Ragtime uses a device called *syncopation* to produce a novel kind of rhythm and melody. Instead of placing an accent on the strong musical beats, syncopation accents the weak beats. The result is a catchy, offbeat sound that audiences loved. Because his music was so popular, Scott Joplin started writing down his tunes. Word of the "Maple Leaf Rag" spread, and a Sedalia music publisher, John Stark, published the piece in 1899. It became one of the best-known pieces of music in America at that time.

Pianist Marcus Roberts said, "Joplin is a bridge between the European approach to composing, where everything is carefully notated, and American music forms. Joplin is the foundation of everything that became jazz. At the same time, he loved classical music and was inspired by European methods to carefully write out his seemingly folk ideas," continued Roberts.[4]

In 1901, Scott Joplin married Belle Hayden and moved to St. Louis. After the great success of the "Maple Leaf Rag," Joplin was earning enough in royalties to live comfortably. He still played piano occasionally, but spent most of his time composing and teaching music. Belle and Scott Joplin had a daughter in 1903, but the child died and the couple separated soon after.

During the summer of 1904, Joplin married Freddie Alexander in Little Rock, Arkansas. The couple went by train back to Sedalia, with Scott Joplin giving concerts in towns along the way. Soon after arriving in Sedalia, Freddie got pneumonia and died, just ten weeks after her wedding. Scott Joplin left Sedalia after Freddie's death and never returned.

Joplin moved to New York City in 1907, where he continued to compose, to teach, and to dream. In 1911, he completed the score of his opera, *Treemonisha,* which is set on an Arkansas plantation in the 1880s. A baby is found abandoned under a tree by Ned and Monisha, who are freed slaves. The tree protected the baby from a fierce storm during the night, so she is named Treemonisha. The child learns to read and grows up to "lead the newly freed slaves out of ignorance and superstition and into the

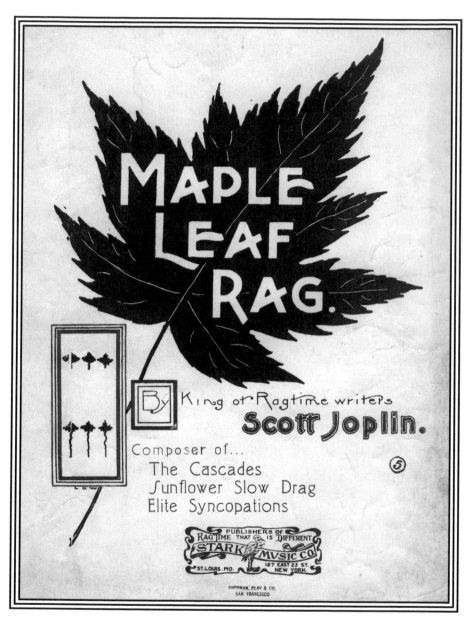

A page from "Maple Leaf Rag" (shown above), which was one of Joplin's most popular compositions.

light of learning."[5] Scott Joplin believed that "racial equality would come with education."[6]

Joplin spent two years working on his opera, but could not find anyone who wanted to produce it. Finally, he used his own money to publish *Treemonisha*, but he never saw a professional performance of the opera. Joplin eventually wrote about sixty compositions including forty more rags, such as "The Entertainer," "Weeping Willow," and "Elite Syncopations." He also wrote several marches, a ballet called "A Ragtime Dance," and two operas, *Guest of Honor* and *Treemonisha*.

Ragtime was losing some of its popularity during the years Scott Joplin lived in New York City. Jazz was taking the music world by storm, leaving behind the steady beat of ragtime. Ragtime had a great deal of influence on the development of jazz, though, even though there is a fundamental difference between the two. Ragtime is written out note for note and requires performers who can read music. Jazz depends on improvisation, which is the ability of its performers to create music as they play. Jazz musicians may or may not be able to play from written notes.

With the decline of ragtime came a decline in Scott Joplin's emotional and physical health. He died in New York City on April 1, 1917, and both he and his music were eventually forgotten, until 1975. That is the year the Houston Grand Opera rescued *Treemonisha* from the dustbin of history. The

Houston production "granted Joplin's profound wish for a professional production of his beloved opera, a dream Joplin didn't see during his lifetime."[7] *Treemonisha* was a great success and Joplin's opera was later produced on Broadway. In 1976, Scott Joplin was posthumously awarded a Pulitzer Prize for music.

It was Hollywood and the movies that brought Scott Joplin's music back to the general public. When Marvin Hamlisch used some of Joplin's rags in the 1973 movie *The Sting*, the public liked the catchy tunes. The movie led to a revival of interest in ragtime and Scott Joplin.

In 1983, ten years after *The Sting* was released, Sedalia, Missouri, began having an annual Scott Joplin Festival. For a week in the spring, musicians and fans gather in the place where Joplin first found fame. They listen to ragtime, tap their feet, and dance a little. One long-time Sedalia resident, Frances Trader, wrote in 1999, "Our week-long celebration of the 100th anniversary of Scott Joplin's "Maple Leaf Rag" is over and it was great. People came from as far away as Canada, Australia, and England."[8]

Gunther Schuller, who conducted a New England orchestra during a Joplin revival in the 1970s, said, "I gave 1,700 performances of his music, and I never got tired of it. I could go into a concert after a horrible day, play four bars of Joplin, and be flying. This is great music, and it will live forever."[9]

3

Charles Ives
(1874–1954)

When Charles Ives was just thirteen years old, he began playing drums in his father's band. A few months later, Charles wrote his first musical composition, a march called "Holiday Quick Step". His father liked the march so much he decided to have the band play it during their next concert. Charles was very shy and refused to take part in the performance. That shyness would be with him for the rest of his life, as far as his music was concerned.

Charles Ives was born in Danbury, Connecticut, on October 20, 1874, to George and Mary Parmelee Ives. His father had been a bandmaster with the Union Army during the Civil War. By the time Charles was born, the Civil War had been over for

Charles Ives

nearly ten years and his father was conducting the local city band and teaching music lessons.

George Ives liked to explore new sounds and unconventional music. As he taught his son to play the piano, cornet, and organ, he also encouraged him to experiment with different sounds. Sometimes George Ives would have Charles and his brother sing a song like "Swanee River" in one key while he played the song on the piano in another key. Charles Ives said his father did this "to stretch our ears and strengthen our musical minds."[1]

Charles spent a lot of time listening to his father's band and other small-town bands. The senior Ives would often separate his band and put some of the musicians in the village square and others in a church steeple or on top of a building. They were all supposed to play the same tune at the same time, but often they got their signals crossed and went their own way. The effect was the same as we feel today when several bands follow each other in a parade, each one playing something different. We recognize snatches from each tune, but the overall effect is a jumble of mixed-up sounds.

At about the same time Charles Ives joined his father's band, he also started playing the organ at the West Street Congregational Church in Danbury. Sometimes Charles worried about spending so much time on music and said, "When other boys on Monday mornings on vacation were out driving the grocery cart, riding horses, or playing ball, I felt all wrong to stay in and play the piano."[2]

Even though Charles Ives spent a great deal of time on music, he also attended school in Danbury and played sports. When he was a teenager, he pitched for the Danbury Alerts, a local baseball team. And he was captain of the Danbury High School football team during his senior year. When people who were interested in his music asked him what he played, Charles usually answered "shortstop."[3]

After graduating from Danbury High School, Charles attended Hopkins Preparatory School in New Haven, Connecticut. In 1894, he entered Yale University, where he studied music composition and organ. He also played football and was on the Yale rowing team during college. After graduating from Yale in 1898 with a bachelor of arts degree, Charles Ives moved to New York City, where his life took a different turn.

Ives went to work as a clerk with the Mutual Life Insurance Company at a salary of five dollars a week. He shared an apartment with some friends and made extra money playing the organ at Central Presbyterian Church. During his years at Mutual, Charles Ives learned about the workings of the insurance business. In 1906, he helped start the insurance firm of Ives and Myrick, where he stayed as senior partner for the next twenty-five years. Music became something Charles Ives had time for only in the evenings and on weekends, but he never lost his desire to compose.

After Ives married Harmony Twichell on June 9, 1908, she said, "He could hardly wait for dinner to be over, and he was at the piano. Often he went to bed at 2 or 3 A.M. Charles Ives added that "we never went anywhere, and she didn't mind." He felt that his wife was a great influence on his music and said, "She urged me on my way to be myself and gave me her confidence."[4] A few years after their marriage, Charles and Harmony adopted a daughter, Edith.

Within a few years, the firm of Ives and Myrick was very successful and began making a great deal of money. In addition to giving the family financial security, Charles Ives explained, "My business experience revealed life to me in many aspects that I might otherwise have missed."[5] He added, "My work in music helped my business, and my work in business helped my music."[6]

Ives continued to go to work every day and compose music in his spare time. He never tried to have any of his music published or performed and only his wife and a few close friends heard any of it. After he wrote a composition, it usually got stuffed in a drawer or closet.

Charles Ives wrote symphonies, chamber music, sonatas, and more than 150 songs. One of his most famous songs was written in honor of William Booth, founder of the Salvation Army. It is called "General William Booth Enters Into Heaven."

In Ives's music there are elements of American popular music such as hymns, marches, and even

Ives's composing was unique. In a note to his copyist about a draft of his sheet music, Ives said, "Mr. Price—please don't try to make things nice! All the wrong notes are <u>right</u>. Just copy as I have—I want it that way."

Ives composed music in this room of his home. He used his piano and Victrola when composing and listening to music.

ragtime. The composer wrote, "I think there must be a soul all made of tunes, of tunes of long ago; I hear the organ on the Main Street corner, Aunt Sarah humming, Gospels . . . the Village cornet band playing in the square."[7]

Unfortunately the music of Charles Ives was not heard by very many people. His Third Symphony, which was written around 1902, was not performed for more than forty years. It was awarded a Pulitzer Prize for music in 1947. In 1951, Leonard Bernstein conducted the premiere of Ives's Second Symphony. Charles Ives was invited to attend the premiere, but turned down the offer. He did listen to the broadcast on a radio in the kitchen of his home and seemed pleased by the performance.

Charles Ives later became known as the first serious American composer to break away from the musical style of the Europeans. He established a new style that was strictly his own. Ives remembered his father's experiments using several bands in different areas, all trying to play the same thing. In some of his works, he did on purpose what had happened accidentally in Danbury. Ives divided an orchestra into three or more parts: one part onstage, one offstage, and another in the balcony. The various sections were told to play their own music in different keys and tempos. The result for the listener was often one of musical chaos.

An example of this technique, called polytonality, is seen in Ives's Fourth Symphony. The strings and trumpets of the onstage orchestra are playing along, when they are interrupted by the offstage violins and harp playing something else. Both orchestras continue to play their own pieces to the end, ignoring each other. Most of the rules of musical composition went out the window when it came to the music of Charles Ives. Ives once said, "I let others keep to their music, and I keep to mine."[8]

Music critic Virgil Thomson said that Ives's music, "comes out in sound less well than it looks on the page . . . . Here one problem is that, because his music received no professional performances at the time he was writing it, Ives lacked a sure sense of what 'worked' instrumentally."[9] The reluctance Charles Ives felt as a boy about having his music performed never left him. He also did not like to be interviewed or have his picture taken. Because of this shyness, his music was unknown to the world. Composer Aaron Copland wrote in his memoirs, "There we were in the 20s searching for a composer from the older generation with an 'American sound,' and here was Charles Ives composing this incredible music—totally unknown to us!"[10]

By 1928, diabetes and several heart attacks forced Charles Ives to stop composing. He retired to his Connecticut farm and became a recluse. He did not read the newspaper and was never interviewed until 1947. He died at Roosevelt Hospital in New York City on May 19, 1954.

George Gershwin

(1898–1937)

February 12, 1924, was a cold, snowy afternoon in New York City. Yet Aeolian Hall was crowded with music lovers who had come to hear Paul Whiteman's Orchestra. After more than two hours of music, the audience was getting restless, and some started to leave. Then, a young native New Yorker walked onto the stage and took his place at the piano.

Paul Whiteman raised his baton and nodded to the clarinetist, Ross Gorman. When Gorman began playing the first few notes of *Rhapsody in Blue*, the audience perked up. Then George Gershwin started to play the piano part. By the end of the piece, fifteen minutes later, the cheering audience

George Gershwin

was on its feet. They were applauding not only the composition, but also Gershwin's fantastic playing.

George Gershwin later said that he had imagined *Rhapsody in Blue* while riding on a train. "I heard it as a musical kaleidoscope of America, of our vast melting pot, of our natural pep, of our blues, of our metropolitan madness."[1] Who was George Gershwin and where did he learn to play the piano like that?

George Gershwin was born Jacob Gershovitz on September 26, 1898, in Brooklyn, New York, to Moshe and Rose Gershovitz. They were immigrants who had come to the United States from Russia in the 1890s. They also had three other children, Arthur, Frances, and Ira. Moshe Gershovitz owned at various times a bakery, restaurant, cigar store, and pool hall. Ira Gershwin once said, "I was the oldest, then came George, then Arthur and last, our sister, Frances . . . . We were always moving. When my father sold a business and started another we would inevitably move to the new neighborhood. George and I once counted over twenty-five different flats and apartments we remembered having lived in during those years."[2]

When George Gershwin was eleven years old, a piano was delivered to one of those apartments. According to Ira, as soon as the piano was set up, "George sat down and played a popular tune of the day. I remember being particularly impressed by his left hand. I had no idea he could play . . . ."[3] George Gershwin had played a friend's piano only a few times, but he seemed to have a natural talent for music.

Before the arrival of the piano, George got into a few scrapes around his various neighborhoods. All that moving around made him the new kid on the block all too often. His brother Ira recalled that George, "would get into fights and come home with black eyes."[4] George said the piano made a difference in his life. "Studying the piano made a good boy out of a bad boy. I was a changed person after I took it up."[5]

George may have stopped fighting, but playing the piano didn't keep him from skipping school a lot. He eventually dropped out of school at age fifteen and became a song plugger in Tin Pan Alley. This was an area in Manhattan where many music publishers had their offices. George worked for some of the companies, playing selections on the piano from the sheet music they had for sale. There were other song pluggers playing for other publishers too. The sound from so many pianos playing at once was sometimes described as being like people banging on tin pans.

In 1916, when George Gershwin was eighteen years old, he got his first song published. It was called "When You Want 'Em You Can't Get 'Em, When You've Got 'Em, You Don't Want 'Em." He got five dollars for the song, which was not much of a start. So he kept on plugging and writing. Three years later, in 1919, Gershwin wrote "Swanee," and was lucky enough to have it introduced by Al Jolson, the well-known singer.

At fifteen, George Gershwin became a "song plugger" in Tin Pan Alley, a music industry section of Manhattan (shown above).

"Swanee" made George Gershwin famous—and rich. His share of the royalties in the first year alone was about $10,000, a small fortune in 1920. He got another big break when he was hired to write the music for a Broadway show, *La, La, Lucille.* The show was a hit and it launched Gershwin on his Broadway career.

In 1921, Ira Gershwin began working with his brother, writing the words to George's songs. For the next fifteen years, George and Ira Gershwin turned out at least one Broadway musical every year. Some of their more successful shows included *Lady Be Good* (1924), *Funny Face* (1927), and *Of Thee I Sing* (1931). Many of the Gershwins' Broadway musicals were adapted for films. George and Ira also composed music for original Hollywood movies such as *Shall We Dance*, starring Fred Astaire and Ginger Rogers, and *Damsel in Distress*, with Fred Astaire and Joan Fontaine.

Yet all the time George Gershwin was writing for Broadway and Hollywood, he had another goal. He wanted to prove to himself and to his audiences that he could write serious concert music. So when Walter Damrosch, conductor of the New York Symphony, asked him in 1925 to write a concerto for piano and orchestra, he jumped at the chance. Concerto in F premiered on December 3, 1925, with Gershwin as the piano soloist. Concerto in F was a success with audiences and critics alike. Conductor Damrosch said of Gershwin, "I think the second movement . . . with its dreamy atmosphere of a summer night . . . reaches a high-water mark of his talent."[6]

The most ambitious project Gershwin ever undertook was his opera, *Porgy and Bess*. In 1926, Gershwin happened to read a novel called *Porgy* by Dubose Heyward. He immediately got in touch with Heyward and said he would like to make the book into an opera. Heyward agreed, but it was almost ten years before George and Ira Gershwin finished the project.

Porgy and Bess opened in New York City on October 10, 1935. The opera tells the story of Porgy, a handicapped black man in Charleston, South Carolina, who got around in a little goat cart. Porgy won, then lost, the love of Bess and killed a man defending his lost love. The opera, which is still performed today, runs for more than three hours, not counting intermissions. It contains such memorable songs as "Summertime" and "It Ain't Necessarily So."

Pianist Herbie Hancock said the music of *Porgy and Bess* "was deeper than just the black experience, and that's why people all over the world can relate to it—it's really about the human spirit."[7] *Porgy and Bess* was later made into a movie with Sidney Poitier playing the role of Porgy.

When he was not writing music, George Gershwin loved to party and entertain his friends. Many thought the self-confident musician had a huge ego. Pianist Oscar Levant teased his friend by saying, "Tell me, George, if you had to do it all over again, would you still fall in love with yourself?"[8] George Gershwin did not marry but was involved with a number of different women. After he became rich and famous, he led a very comfortable life in his Manhattan apartment. He often composed music late at night while watching the twinkling lights of New York City from his windows.

George Gershwin's life was cut short by a brain tumor. The talented composer died on July 11, 1937, in Los Angeles, California, at the age of thirty-eight. Sixty years later, singer Tony Bennett said, "I'll never forget, I was playing a club in Beverly Hills a while ago, and there were all youngsters in the audience, really, really young kids. And when I got to 'They Can't Take That Away From Me,' all the young people sang the song with me . . . . Gershwin's music never goes out of fashion, it's as alive today as it was when it first came out."[9]

5

Duke Ellington
(1899–1974)

Duke Ellington wrote in his autobiography, "About this time, too, just before I went to high school, and before my voice broke, I got my nickname, Duke. I had a chum, Edgar McEntree . . . a rather fancy guy who liked to dress well. He was socially uphill and a pretty good, popular fellow around with parties and that sort of thing. I think he felt that in order for me to be eligible for his constant companionship, I should have a title. So he named me Duke."[1] In time, Duke Ellington certainly lived up to his name.

Duke was born Edward Kennedy Ellington in Washington, D.C., on April 29, 1899. His father, James Edward Ellington, made blueprints for the Department of the Navy during the day. At night he

Duke Ellington

worked as a White House butler. Daisy Kennedy Ellington was a homemaker and mother to Duke and his sister, Ruth. The Ellington family was very religious. Duke said, "I didn't go to one church each Sunday. I went to two. My mother was a Baptist and my father a Methodist."[2]

Duke started playing the family piano when he was just seven years old. He also took piano lessons and said, "My piano teacher, Mrs. Clinkscales (that was really her name), got paid several times a week for many weeks for those lessons, but I missed more than I took, because of my enthusiasm for playing ball, and running and racing through the street. That I remember very well, because when she had her piano recital with all her pupils in the church, I was the only one who could not play his part."[3]

Duke went to school in Washington and said, "School went all right, I suppose, because I made my grades in spite of my enthusiasm for baseball."[4] Duke also worked at a soda fountain after school and named his first musical composition, "Soda Fountain Rag." Music wasn't Duke's only talent. He won an art contest sponsored by the National Association for the Advancement of Colored People (NAACP) during his senior year in high school.

After Ellington won the contest, the Pratt Institute of Applied Arts in Brooklyn, New York, offered him a scholarship. Instead of going to school, he took a job playing in a band at night and worked as a commercial artist during the day. Ellington had met the girl of his dreams and worked day and night to save enough money to marry Edna Thompson in 1918.

It turned out that 1918 was a big year for Duke Ellington! In addition to his marriage, it was the year he formed his first jazz band, called Duke's Serenaders. For five years, the band played in the Washington, D.C., area before moving to New York City. Beginning with ten members, the band eventually grew to thirty members. Duke's Serenaders revolutionized the idea of a jazz band. Instead of a small combo of four or five men who probably could not read music, Duke's band was a professional orchestra. The musicians had to know how to read music as well as how to improvise and create new sounds.

After playing in various clubs in New York and New England, the band began a five-year stint at the Cotton Club in Harlem, from 1927 until 1931. Even though it was segregated, many African-American musicians got their start at the famous New York dance club. African Americans were allowed only in the bands, not in the audience. During his five years at the Cotton Club, Duke Ellington wrote his first big hit, "Mood Indigo."

Ellington left the Cotton Club and started the Duke Ellington Orchestra in 1931. In 1933, he took the band on a very successful European tour. In Europe, Duke was accepted as a first-class composer and performer and played in concert halls. Back in

America, the band had to be satisfied with jobs in night clubs and dance halls. But that would change.

By 1943, right in the middle of World War II, Duke and his band played in New York's Carnegie Hall. It is here that Ellington's great long composition, *Black, Brown and Beige*, was played for the first time. The work is subtitled: "A Tonal Parallel to the History of the Negro in America." It is Ellington's most ambitious work, consisting of seven movements that relate musically the problems black people face when growing up in a racist society. After twenty years of night clubs and dance halls, Duke's band had finally played in America's most famous concert hall.

The band continued to perform many concerts in America and Europe during the next fifteen years. Ellington took his sixteen-year-old nephew on one of the European tours in 1959. Michael James sailed first-class with his famous uncle and ate at the captain's table several times during the voyage. Many of the other first-class passengers asked Duke Ellington to play something for them.

According to his nephew Michael, "Duke didn't have the whole band on the ship, because some of the guys had decided to fly over, but on the last night he gathered the seven guys who were with him, and they played for the captain and the people an impromptu jam performance. But being a true democrat, once Duke had done that he had to go to all of the classes. He went to play for the cabin class, then for the tourist class, and he wound up in the crew's quarters. That's how he was about not leaving anybody out. He used to say, 'I never put anybody in a secondary position.'"[5]

Back in America, Duke's band played at the Newport Jazz Festival in Newport, Rhode Island. The high point of the evening was Duke's composition, "Diminuendo and Crescendo in Blue." His tenor sax player, Paul Gonsalves, played a chorus, then another and another until he had played *twenty-seven* choruses. The audience went wild! The concert put Newport on the map and Ellington on the cover of *Time* magazine. *Ellington at Newport* became the Duke's all-time best-selling recording.

With success after success piling up, Duke Ellington was invited to Hollywood. It was there he wrote the music for the movie *Anatomy of a Murder,* starring James Stewart and George C. Scott as opposing lawyers in a murder trial. This film, one of director Otto Preminger's finest, won Ellington three Grammy Awards. But, like so many other composers of popular music, Duke Ellington wanted to write serious music.

Ellington composed three *Sacred Concerts* for Grace Episcopal Cathederal in San Francisco in 1965, the Cathedral of St. John the Divine in New York in 1968, and for London's Westminster Abbey in 1973. A group of ministers condemned the first of these concerts. They were scandalized by the idea of a nightclub musician playing in church.

Duke Ellington wowed audiences with his music and style. His sizzling performance in Newport, Rhode Island landed him on the cover of *Time* magazine.

Duke Ellington wrote in 1973, in reference to the second *Sacred Concert,* "I regard this concert as the most important thing I have ever done."[6] The *Sacred Concerts* contain some of Ellington's most impressive music. While the jazz instrumental style is heard throughout the concerts, there are also many passages of quiet devotion. Most feature a mixed choir, singing with or without instrumental accompaniment, and sometimes just speaking in unison. Duke touchingly said of his sacred music, "Now I can say openly what I have been saying on my knees."[7]

In 1969, Duke Ellington was awarded the Presidential Medal of Freedom. At the first all jazz party at the White House, President Richard Nixon presented the medal to Ellington. Then the president sat down at the piano and led the audience in a chorus of "Happy Birthday" in honor of Ellington's seventieth birthday.

During the ceremony, Duke Ellington took the microphone and said, "I am reminded of the Four Freedoms . . . . freedom from hate . . . . freedom from all self-pity . . . freedom from fear of doing something that might help another more than himself, and freedom from the kind of pride that could make a man feel he was better than his brother or neighbor."[8]

Duke Ellington continued to tour with his band until poor health forced him to stop. When he was in the hospital during his last illness, he had a piano delivered to his room so he could continue writing music. Duke Ellington died on May 24, 1974.

Ellington's granddaughter, Mercedes Ellington, said "My grandfather saw himself an instrument of God. Just like he always kept a piano nearby, there was always a Bible, too."[9]

Duke Ellington's son, Mercer, took over and directed the orchestra until his own death in 1997. Mercer's son Paul, who is Duke Ellington's grandson, is the current director of the orchestra. Shelly Carroll, a tenor sax player under Mercer for more than ten years, said, "Every time I play his [Duke's] music, I hear something different and fresh and beautiful. That is the definition of great music."[10]

Aaron Copland

6

Aaron Copland
(1900–1990)

The subway was running late. Aaron Copland raced across New York City on his way to Aeolian Hall. The New York Symphony Orchestra was rehearsing Copland's first symphony in the hall. He explained, "I was in such a hurry that instead of going around the block to the stage entrance, I yanked open the front door. Suddenly, I got a blast of my own orchestration! It was a moment I shall never forget. It sounded so glorious to me, so much grander than I could possibly have imagined."[1]

Aaron Copland, who is often called the Dean of American Music, was born in Brooklyn, New York, on November 14, 1900, the youngest of five children. His parents, Harris and Sarah Mittenthal

Copland, were Russian-Jewish immigrants. Although the family owned a piano, only Aaron had a serious interest in music. He learned basic piano skills from his older sister, Laurine. Soon she had taught him all she knew, and when Aaron was four-teen, he asked to take piano lessons from a neighborhood teacher. He later said, "I distinctly remember with what fear and trembling I knocked on the door of Mr. Leopold Wolfsohn's piano studio on Clinton Avenue in Brooklyn and . . . arranged for piano lessons."[2]

At the age of fifteen, Aaron attended his first concert, a recital by the great Polish pianist, Ignaz Jan Paderewski. He decided then and there to become a composer. During his senior year at Boys' High School in Brooklyn, he began studying harmony, composition, and counterpoint with Rubin Goldmark. During the four years he spent with Goldmark, Aaron Copland carefully saved his money. He had heard that a music school for Americans was being established in Fontainebleau, France, and he hoped to go there.

In 1921, Copland received a scholarship from the Conservatoire Americain and moved to France. He studied musical composition with Paul Vidal. Copland went with Vidal to visit a composition class taught in Paris by Madame Nadia Boulanger. He was so impressed with her, and she with him, that Copland moved to Paris and spent the next three years studying with Boulanger.

Aaron Copland returned to New York in 1924 and found work as a pianist with a trio that played in a Mitford, Pennsylvania, resort. He played the piano at night and during the day worked on a symphony for organ and orchestra that Nadia Boulanger asked him to write. She wanted to use the composition during her upcoming American tour as an organist with the New York and Boston symphonies. The first performance of the Organ Symphony took place on January 11, 1925, in New York's Aeolian Hall. Unfortunately, the Organ Symphony, like most of Copland's early works, failed to catch on with the concert-going public.

One of the pieces that eventually made his reputation as a composer was *El Salón México*. In 1932, Copland spent four months in Mexico City. During his time there, he listened to a lot of the local music, including mariachi bands and folk singers. He said, "Mexico has turned out even grander than I expected and I expected pretty grand things."[3] Copland was so captivated by what he heard, he immediately began work on *El Salón México*, which was based on the sounds of Mexican folk tunes. He finished the composition in 1936 and it was premiered by the Mexico Symphony Orchestra in 1937. It was an immediate success in Mexico and later in the United States. The popularity of the piece gave Copland the encouragement to continue composing.

In the space of the next seven years, Copland composed three ballets, *Billy the Kid* in 1938, *Rodeo* in 1942, and *Appalachian Spring* in 1944. *Billy the Kid* is based on the very short life of the desperado Henry McCarty, alias William Bonney. Bonney called himself Billy and reputedly shot one man for each of his twenty-one years. He was finally gunned down by his former friend, Sheriff Pat Garrett. Copland made use of several well-known cowboy songs as part of the ballet's music, including "The Old Chisholm Trail" and "Old Paint." The day after *Billy the Kid* opened in New York City, there was a line of people four blocks long waiting to buy tickets. Copland said, "I cannot remember another work of mine that was so unanimously well received."[4]

He got the same response with *Rodeo.* The premiere at the Metropolitan Opera on October 16, 1942, was sold out. After the show's last great number, "Hoe-Down," the audience responded with a standing ovation and many curtain calls. *Appalachian Spring* also got rave reviews and won a Pulitzer Prize for Aaron Copland in 1945.

In 1961, years after the premiere of *Rodeo,* Aaron Copland was scheduled to conduct the Tuscon Symphony Orchestra. He planned to visit music publicist Eleanor Spector while he was in Arizona. She recalled, "I was expecting him early on a Sunday afternoon, and he didn't arrive. Time went by. Finally he showed up that evening and I said to him, 'Where have you been?' He laughed . . . and told me he'd been to a rodeo in Tucson. I said, 'But you already wrote *Rodeo,* and you captured the feeling of it!' And he said, 'But I'd never been to a rodeo. How could I not go?'"[5]

In addition to his ballets, Aaron Copland wrote many other successful compositions. *Fanfare for the Common Man*, which premiered right in the middle of World War II, became one of his most popular and most played works. It was written to raise spirits during the dark days of the war and has served ever since as a kind of victory anthem for America.

Another of Copland's wartime compositions was his *Lincoln Portrait*, written for orchestra and narrator. It included parts of Abraham Lincoln's speeches and had its premiere in 1942. Copland explained, "In the opening section, I wanted to suggest something of the mysterious sense of fatality that surrounds Lincoln's personality. Also . . . something of his gentleness and simplicity of spirit. The . . . middle section briefly sketches in the background of the times he lived (the Civil War). This merges into the concluding section, where my sole purpose was to draw a simple but impressive frame about the words of Lincoln himself."[6] The production ends with a narrator reading from the last part of the *Gettysburg Address*: " . . . that we here highly resolve that these dead shall not have died in vain . . . that government of the people, by the people, and for the people shall not perish from the earth."[7]

Like both George Gershwin and Duke Ellington, Aaron Copland also spent some time in Hollywood, where the big money was. He composed music for

Aaron Copland (right) received many awards in recognition for his work. Here he is accepting an award from Edgard Varèse, a fellow composer.

several movies, including *Of Mice and Men*, *The Red Pony*, and *Our Town*. In addition to composing music, Aaron Copland wrote three books: *What to Listen for in Music* in 1939, *Music and Imagination* in 1952, and *Copland on Music* in 1960.

Sometimes Aaron Copland was criticized for his music. He did not let that stop him, though. He went on composing for fifty years. He lived for his music. He sat for hours at his piano, jotting down note after note, experimenting, checking, erasing, rearranging—until he got it the way he wanted it.

Copland biographer Howard Pollack wrote, "Copland hoped to create an American classical music that was serious and widely accepted."[8]

Aaron Copland stopped composing music in the 1970s, but he continued to conduct. In a 1977 interview, he said, "I've bogged down a bit. I might start up again, but I am seventy-seven years old and most composers didn't have the luck to live that long, so they didn't have the problem of going on. When you've been composing for more than fifty years it gives you quite a long time to express yourself."[9] Aaron Copland died on December 2, 1990, at the age of ninety.

In the year 2000, there were celebrations across America celebrating the 100th anniversary of Aaron Copland's birth. Conductor Mischa Semanitzky said many of Copland's works such as *Billy the Kid* and *Rodeo* are "so striking and so western, you can feel the plains. Pretty good for a Brooklyn boy."[10]

Samuel Barber

7

Samuel Barber
(1910–1981)

There were good musical genes in the Barber family, and Samuel inherited most of them. He was born on March 10, 1910, in West Chester, Pennsylvania, to Samuel and Marguerite McLeod Barber. Samuel's father was a doctor and his mother a pianist. His mother's sister, Louise Homer, was a famous singer with the Metropolitan Opera in New York City. Her husband, Sidney Homer, was a composer whose songs were popular at the time. Samuel attended his first opera at the age of six, to hear his aunt sing the role of Amneris in *Aida*, opposite the famous Enrico Caruso as Radames.

By this time, Samuel was picking out little pieces on the piano, tunes that his mother helped him write down. At seven, he was writing down the songs himself, including one he dedicated to his mother. When Samuel was twelve, he started playing the organ at Westminster Presbyterian Church in West Chester, earning one hundred dollars a month. His musical talents continued to develop, and at age fourteen, Samuel was accepted as one of the first students at the Curtis Institute of Music in Philadelphia.

Even though his parents and relatives were proud of their musical prodigy, they also encouraged him to take part in sports. Samuel wrote a letter to his mother in which he said, "To begin with, I was not meant to be an athlete. I was meant to be a composer, and will be, I'm sure . . . . Don't ask me to try to forget this and go play football. Please!"[1] Barber further explained in a 1978 interview, "I was supposed to be a doctor. I was supposed to go to Princeton. And everything I was supposed to do, I didn't."[2]

Samuel Barber was a very serious student, both in high school and at Curtis, where he studied piano, voice, music theory, and composition. While attending West Chester High School, Samuel organized a small orchestra. He also managed to attend the Friday afternoon concerts of the Philadelphia Orchestra. Barber graduated from high school in 1926. In 1934, he was awarded a bachelor of music degree from Curtis.

While Barber was still at Curtis, his uncle Sidney told him to ignore the latest musical fads and follow his own tastes. "Opinions don't change a note or add

Barber had many musical influences as a child. His mother was a
pianist. His uncle was a composer and his aunt was a famous opera
singer. He wrote his first composition at the age of seven.

to your stature. The only thing to do is to get down to brass tacks and fight the thing out on your own line, doing, as nearly as you can, the thing that you know you want to do."[3] Barber took his uncle's advice and said many years later, "I myself wrote always as I wished."[4]

Barber traveled to Europe for the first time in the summer of 1928, when he was eighteen years old. He attended many concerts, operas, and ballets while abroad. After returning to school in the fall, Barber finished a Sonata for Violin that he had started composing in Europe. The piece won a $1,200 Bearns Prize in 1928, which was awarded by Columbia University.

On another European trip in 1931, Barber wrote his first composition for full orchestra, the Overture to *The School for Scandal.* It was based on a play by Richard Brinsley Sheridan, a seventeenth century English dramatist. The "comedy of manners" ridiculed the proper behavior, social intrigue, and malicious gossip of the time. The composition had its premiere in 1933 and won another Bearns Prize for Barber.

A streak of sadness is seen in many of Barber's works, including *Dover Beach*, which he composed in 1931. It is based on the Matthew Arnold poem, *Dover Beach*, which was written in 1869. This composition is one of Barber's most famous works.

Up until 1932, Samuel Barber's style had been very traditional. With his Sonata for Cello and Piano,

Barber's style changed to one of extremely fast tempos and sudden changes in mood. The piece took several years to catch on with performers and the public, but it eventually became popular. His compositions continued to win prizes, and by 1935, Samuel Barber was recognized as one of the greatest composers of serious music in America.

In 1936, Barber completed his first symphony, the Symphony in One Movement. This was followed in 1937 by his String Quartet in B minor. Arturo Toscanini, one of the greatest conductors of all time, asked Barber to rearrange the slow movement of the quartet for a full string orchestra. Toscanini then featured the composition on his radio broadcast with the NBC Symphony on November 5, 1938.

The newly named Adagio for Strings, Op. 11 which is about eight minutes long, became the most popular of all Barber's works. It was played at the funerals of such well-known people as President Franklin Roosevelt, Albert Einstein, and Princess Grace of Monaco. "Because Adagio for Strings has been associated so often with the death of a prominent person, it has been called our national funeral music."[5]

Barber's career took a detour in 1943, when he was inducted into the U.S. Army. He was transferred to the Army Air Forces and instead of going into battle, Barber was asked to write a symphony honoring the military. His lifelong companion, composer Gian Carlo Menotti, once said that "Barber was probably the only soldier in the United States who never learned to take a gun apart and put it together again."[6]

Barber's Symphony No. 2 was dedicated to the Army Air Forces and was first performed by the Boston Symphony Orchestra in March 1944. A week later, the entire performance was transmitted on short wave radio to the world by the Office of War Information.

After the end of World War II in 1945, Barber spent much of his time at Capricorn, a house he bought in 1943 that was located near Mt. Kisco, New York. He shared Capricorn with Gian Carlo Menotti for thirty years. There were two studios at opposite ends of the house so each musician could work and not bother the other one. Barber and Menotti lived at Capricorn until 1973, when the house was sold. They then moved to an apartment in New York City.

In 1945, the conductor of the Boston Symphony, asked Barber to compose a Concerto for Cello and Orchestra. Barber was fortunate because his soloist, the brilliant Russian-born cellist Raya Garbousova, was not afraid to tackle anything. Another famous cellist, Leonard Rose, said it was one of the most difficult concertos he had ever played. Garbousova and the Boston Symphony premiered the composition on April 5, 1946. Even though a Boston critic called it "nervous music," the piece received the Music Critics Circle Award.

No work could show off Barber as a composer like his 1949 Piano Sonata. At least half of the reason for its success lay in the fact that the first performances were played by Vladimir Horowitz, one of the greatest pianists of all time. After hearing a Horowitz concert in Houston, Texas, a reviewer wrote, "Horowitz is always intense, lavishing loving care on every single note as though it were an only child, but he is often at his most intense when he is playing so softly as to be almost inaudible."[7] The last movement of the sonata, which was suggested by Horowitz himself, was written by Barber to take advantage of the great pianist's amazing technique.

After the Horowitz performances of the sonata, Barber had another great triumph in his opera, *Vanessa*. It was his first attempt at grand opera, and was premiered by the New York Metropolitan Opera in 1958. Gian Carlo Menotti wrote the words to go along with Barber's music. The opera, a great popular and critical success, won a Pulitzer Prize for music in 1959. Barber got a second Pulitzer Prize for music in 1963 for his first piano concerto.

Samuel Barber worked slowly while composing his music. According to his publisher, Hans Heinsheimer, each finished page of Barber's music was "a model of perfection. It is not only checked meticulously for errors . . . it is also written very clearly . . . and it is completely ready for the copyist and the printer."[8] Barber seemed to live in a world of music. Biographer Nathan Broder said, "He has been seen in a train drawing staves and writing notes in the air with his fingers and erasing them with a sweep of the hand."[9]

Samuel Barber died on January 23, 1981, in New York City. He was buried next to his mother in the family plot at Oaklands Cemetery in his hometown of West Chester, Pennsylvania.

8

Leonard Bernstein
(1918–1990)

Leonard Bernstein was sound asleep, early Sunday morning, November 14, 1943. The night before he had played the piano in a friend's recital, and then stayed at a party until the early hours. When the phone rang, a groggy Bernstein answered it.

On the line was Bruno Zurato, associate manager of the New York Philharmonic Orchestra. Zurato said the scheduled conductor, Bruno Walter, was sick with the flu and he wanted Bernstein to conduct the 3 P.M. concert. At that time, Leonard Bernstein was an assistant conductor of the Philharmonic, but he had never rehearsed the afternoon's performance with the orchestra. In spite of this, he crawled out of bed, got dressed, and went to the theater.

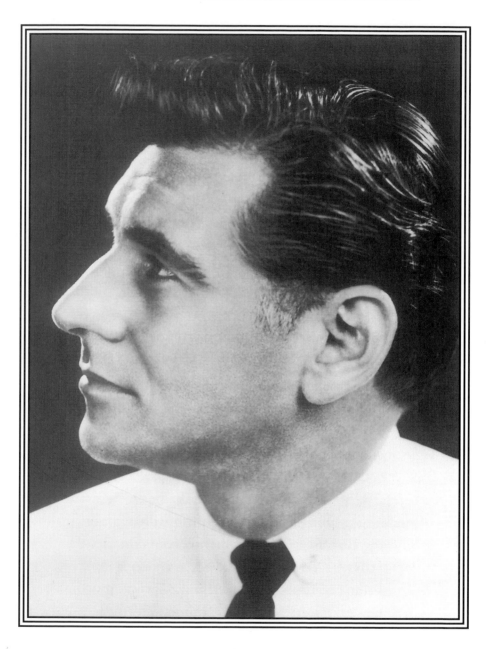

Leonard Bernstein

At the beginning of the concert, the manager announced to the audience that Leonard Bernstein would be filling in for the regular conductor. The audience groaned because they had come to hear Walter. Two hours later, when Bernstein finished the program, the audience rose to its feet and cheered. Critics called the performance sensational, and to make it even better, the concert was broadcast all over the country on CBS radio. It was a lucky break for twenty-five-year-old Leonard Bernstein, whose early years gave little indication of his future fame.

Samuel and Jennie Resnick Bernstein were Russian immigrants who lived in Boston. Their son Leonard was born on August 25, 1918, in Lawrence, Massachusetts, while the family was visiting relatives. In Boston, Samuel owned a beauty supply company. The Bernsteins were also the parents of two more children, Shirley and Burton. Since the Bernstein family moved often, Leonard had a hard time making friends. He later explained, "I was a miserable, terrified little child."[1] Problems with asthma and allergies also made it hard for Leonard to run and play with other children. He grew up lonely and shy.

Leonard's parents enjoyed playing popular music on the record player and radio, but neither knew very much about classical music. The family did not have a piano, but when they visited friends who did, Leonard went straight to the piano and plinked away on the keys. When he was ten years old, his aunt gave her old piano to the family to store for her. He recalled, "I touched it and went mad."[2] From that time on, Leonard spent hours every day practicing.

He found a piano teacher in the neighborhood who charged one dollar for each lesson. After that teacher moved away, Leonard found another teacher, but had to pay three dollars for each lesson, which was nearly his whole allowance. Leonard soon knew more than his second teacher and had to look for a new one. His third teacher was Helen Coates. She encouraged Leonard to attend concerts and listen to classical music. Coates remembered that Leonard "was frighteningly gifted. He absorbed in one lesson an arrangement that took most of my pupils five or six lessons to learn."[3]

When Leonard was eleven years old, he enrolled in the Boston Latin School, where he rose to the top of his class. His success at school and his talent for music helped give Leonard confidence. As a result of his new confidence, Leonard's health also improved. He said, "One day I was a scrawny little thing that everybody could beat up, and the next time I looked around I was the biggest boy in class. I could run faster, jump higher, dive better than everybody."[4]

After graduation from the Boston Latin School in 1935, Leonard Bernstein entered Harvard College. He studied counterpoint, music theory, and music history in addition to his regular academic subjects. Bernstein also played the piano for the school choir and wrote the music for many of Harvard's stage productions.

He graduated with honors in 1939 with a bachelor of arts degree in music. While at Harvard, Bernstein had begun to compose serious music, including a violin/piano sonata and some other piano pieces.

After his graduation from Harvard, Leonard Bernstein was faced with a problem. A guest conductor of the Boston Symphony, Dimitri Mitropoulos, encouraged Bernstein to become a conductor. Leonard's father wanted him to take over the family business in Boston. Since Bernstein had no interest in business, he left home and moved to New York City. He hoped to find work there as a musician but did not have any luck. After a year of unemployment, Mitropoulos helped Bernstein get a scholarship to the Curtis Institute of Music in Philadelphia, Pennsylvania, where he studied conducting for the next two years.

Then, on his twenty-fifth birthday, Leonard Bernstein was offered the job of assistant conductor of the New York Philharmonic Orchestra. This position led to his stunning performance as a substitute conductor on November 14, 1943. After that one concert, Leonard Bernstein had it made. He was suddenly in demand for guest appearances with some of the most famous orchestras in the country.

In 1951, Leonard Bernstein married Felicia Montealegre, an actress from Chile. They lived in an apartment across the street from Carnegie Hall in New York City. Their daughter Jamie was born in 1952, followed by son Alexander in 1955, and daughter Nina in 1962. In a 1999 interview, Jamie

Bernstein Thomas said, "There was always music in the house, there were always musicians in the house. My earliest impressions of grown-ups was this gaggle of incredibly loud, raucous, funny people who spent all their time making a racket and being hilarious and singing at the piano . . . ."[5]

But life in the Bernstein house was not all fun and games according to Jamie. Her father often had trouble switching from being a conductor to being a composer. Leonard Bernstein said, "It is impossible for me to make an exclusive choice among the various activities of conducting, symphonic composition, writing for the theater, or playing the piano. What seems right for me at any given moment is what I must do."[6] No matter what he was doing, Leonard Bernstein did it with his whole being. When he was composing music, he often slept only two or three hours a night. He threw himself into his conducting with vigor also, waving his arms around, jumping into the air, and even falling off of the podium occasionally.

Leonard Bernstein did not compose only classical music. He also wrote music for Broadway and the movies. His first Broadway hit was the 1944 musical *On the Town*, which is about three sailors on leave in New York City. That was followed by musicals, including *Wonderful Town* in 1953 and *West Side Story* in 1957, and the movie *On the Waterfront* in 1954.

Of all of Bernstein's musicals, *West Side Story* is the best known. As a modern-day retelling of Shakespeare's *Romeo and Juliet*, the play is about gang

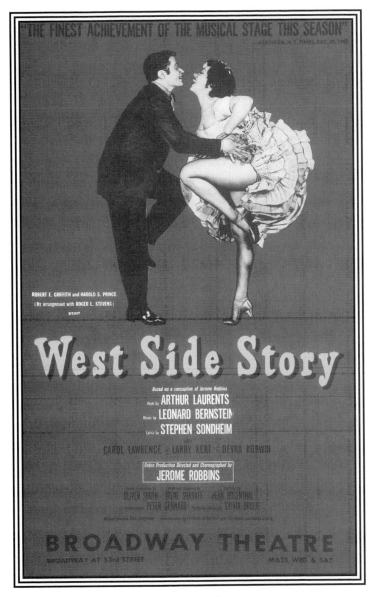

This is a promotional poster for *West Side Story*. The musical was first performed in 1957.

rivalry between the Jets and the Sharks in New York City. Maria, who is the Juliet figure, is a Puerto Rican girl from New York's lower West Side. Tony, who plays the role of Romeo, kills a gang member and then is killed in revenge. After the killings, the Jets and the Sharks are sad and ashamed of the tragedy they created.

A real-life tragedy led Bernstein to dedicate the premiere of his Symphony No. 3 to the recently assassinated President John F. Kennedy in 1963. The work, which is also called *Kaddish*, is based on a Jewish prayer. It premiered in Tel Aviv, and after the performance, Israeli Prime Minister Golda Meir came backstage to congratulate Bernstein on his performance.

The Kennedy Center for the Performing Arts in Washington, D.C., is named for John F. Kennedy. Leonard Bernstein was asked to compose the music for the center's opening in 1971. He wrote a musical that was a combination of classical and pop music based on a Catholic Mass. "*Mass* required some 200 musicians, actors and dancers . . . . and street people, a brass band and a rock band on stage . . . and music issuing from speakers throughout the house."[7] Even though *Mass* was quite a large and elaborate production, it got mixed reviews by the critics.

All the time he was composing these and other works, Leonard Bernstein was equally busy conducting. He became co-conductor of the New York Philharmonic in 1957. He advanced to the position of principal conductor the following year, a post he held for eleven years. He retired from the Philharmonic in 1969 to devote more time to composing. In addition to his classical and popular compositions, Bernstein became one of the most respected music educators of his time.

From 1958 until 1972, he directed a series of fifty-three "Young People's Concerts," which were televised by CBS. His daughter Jamie remembers going to the first concert in Carnegie Hall. "I was 5 and didn't understand a thing. But my brother and sister and I gradually came to think that he was writing the young people's concerts to us. When I became obsessed with the Beatles, Beatles music crept into the young people's concerts."[8] In 1993, twenty-five of the broadcasts were transferred to video and are often used in schools to teach music.

Bernstein once said, "Music is something terribly special. It doesn't have to pass the censor of the brain before it can reach the heart."[9] Leonard Bernstein died on October 14, 1990, in New York City at the age of seventy-two. Six days before he died, he announced that he was retiring because of health problems. There was a private funeral for the family and a few friends. Early in his career, he was urged to change his name to something "more American." He replied, "I'll do it as Bernstein, or not at all."[10]

Philip Glass

Philip Glass
(1937–)

In 1978, when Philip Glass was forty-one years old, he was driving a taxi in New York City. At various times in his life he had also been a plumber, airport baggage handler, crane operator, and furniture mover. After work though, he always returned to his real interest, which was composing music.

Philip was born in Baltimore, Maryland, on January 31, 1937, to Benjamin and Ida Gouline Glass. His father owned a small radio repair and record shop, and his mother was a schoolteacher and librarian. Philip recalled, "I hauled records around from as early as I can remember. We sold mostly top-40 stuff and, though I knew it all, I thought it was pretty much junk. We took home the records we didn't sell and a lot of it was chamber music. That's what I really listened to."[1]

Philip taught himself to play the piano by listening as his older brother and sister took their lessons. By the time he was six years old, he was also taking violin lessons. The violin did not really interest him, though, so he began studying flute at the Peabody Conservatory in Baltimore when he was eight. Philip went to public school in Baltimore and played the flute in the school band. He graduated from high school in 1952 at the age of fifteen and enrolled in the University of Chicago. In college, he studied mathematics and philosophy and earned a bachelor of arts degree in 1956, when he was nineteen years old.

Philip Glass wanted to go to New York City to study at the Juilliard School of Music, but he did not have the money. He worked for several months as a crane operator and saved $1,200, which was enough to get started at Juilliard. During the next five years, he wrote and studied music and heard about seventy-five of his compositions performed at the school. Glass earned a master's degree in music from Juilliard in 1962.

He was then hired to be a composer-in-residence for the Pittsburgh, Pennsylvania, public schools from 1962 to 1964. During these years, he found that composing was becoming more and more difficult. "I had reached a kind of dead end with music. I couldn't do it anymore. Not that I couldn't; I could turn it out easily. That was the problem. I just didn't believe in it anymore."[2]

So there he was, at the age of twenty-seven, burned out. After talking to his friends and teachers, Glass decided to go to Paris and study with Nadia Boulanger. She was seventy-eight at the time and had taught some of the world's most famous musicians. According to Philip Glass, "Boulanger believed that the training we got in America was simply not thorough enough. She was convinced that at age 27 I had to redo completely my musical education."[3] For two years he studied counterpoint and harmony with the famous teacher. He made a little money by working as an extra in movies.

While Glass was working in the movies, he met the famous Indian master of the sitar, Ravi Shankar. Glass was fascinated with the almost hypnotic rhythm of Shankar's exotic Eastern music. From that time on, Glass began to use the best elements of the music of the East and the West in his own compositions. He said, "Overnight I began writing a completely different kind of music."[4] "I wanted to create music that spoke to me emotionally. I wanted my own voice."[5]

In 1967, Philip Glass returned to New York City and began writing his own brand of music. The name given to most of his compositions was *minimalism.* This is a style that uses a steady tempo along with simple melodies and harmonies that are repeated over and over. Glass based his compositions on a combination of Indian and classical music, African drumming, and even rock and roll. At the time Glass began composing in this style, there was not much of an audience for his music. In order to promote his new sound, Glass and six other musicians formed the Philip Glass Ensemble in 1968.

Glass's first work to gain much notice was *Music in 12 Parts*, which he wrote especially for his own ensemble. Reception to the 1974 premiere of *Music in 12 Parts* was mostly very cool. Various critics described the piece as stuck-record music, trance music; they even called it hypnotically repetitive. Other critics, though, thought the piece was a major accomplishment. Even though some of the reviews were negative, Philip Glass was finally getting some attention.

The following year, the Paris premiere of the Glass opera, *Einstein On the Beach*, also attracted much attention. The four-and-a-half-hour opera has no intermissions. It is designed to show the importance of Albert Einstein, from the time he was a little boy to the development of his theory of relativity. Einstein is represented by a number of different characters. In one scene his character is writing mathematical formulas on a blackboard. In another he is shown sitting in a spaceship.

Many of the actors in the opera speak nonsense phrases or count in a sing-song chant. Some of the characters appear to be in a trance. Props include "a train that turns into a cellblock, dancers in a glade, a rocket ship in the sky . . . and an aged violinist off to one side dressed as—of course—Professor Einstein."[6] In spite of its unusual style, the opera was a sensation and was performed all over Europe during the next few months. *Einstein On the Beach* was awarded an Obie, which is an Off-Broadway prize, in 1975.

Glass later said, "It was really when I began working on my own pieces in the middle '70s, beginning with *Einstein on the Beach*, that I really began to think seriously about just what the pieces were about. Or to put it another way, when you start to write an opera . . . it can take about a year and a half to do a small piece, and a large piece may take as long as three years. So, for me to spend that much time working on a project, it has to be about something that is important to me."[7]

Glass composed another opera in 1984, called *Akhnaten*, after the Egyptian pharaoh who ruled from 1397 to 1362 B.C. The pharaoh tried unsuccessfully to introduce to his world the idea of worshipping only one god, in this case the sun. The opera is sung in three ancient languages, Egyptian, Babylonian, and Hebrew. In addition, the narrator speaks the language of the country where the opera is performed.

The music of *Akhnaten* contains the usual almost endless repetition of certain melodies. But there are also very traditional passages for soloists, large chorus, and orchestra. After the premiere of *Akhnaten*, Glass admitted, "There may be people out there who still don't like my music, but I don't think they can ignore it any longer."[8] American theater director Robert Wilson said, "Phil has a keen visual sense and a profound understanding of drama and theater . . . . Because of him, all kinds of people who thought opera was something that belonged in the 19th century have come to appreciate it."[9]

Philip Glass has had three wives. He married actress Jo Ann Akalaitis in the 1960s and had two children with her, Julie and Zachary. The couple divorced and Glass married a physician, Luba Burtyk. After their divorce, Glass married Candy Jernigan, who died in 1991.

In the late 1990s, Glass was asked to compose music for the 1931 classic horror movie, *Dracula*. At the time it was made, *Dracula* was a silent movie. Glass wrote the soundtrack and then went on tour with the movie during the Halloween season in 2000. As the old black-and-white movie flickered on the screen, Philip Glass and the orchestra played the music live. He said, "*Dracula* is fun. We wear fangs on stage sometimes."[10] He added, "For someone who works in the world of classical music, the film provides you with an audience which is tremendously bigger than you normally get."[11] Philip Glass has also written music for television commercials and other movies in addition to his classical works.

In a 1992 interview, Philip Glass said to those who were struggling to become composers, "Take pleasure in what you're doing—for many years that

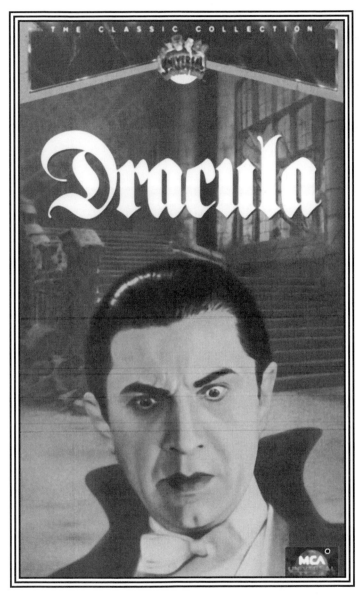

Philip Glass composed music to accompany the classic 1931 horror movie *Dracula*. This is a recreation of a poster for the silent movie starring Bela Lugosi.

may be the only reward you're going to get! If you don't rejoice in it you are going to have a very hard time. You can't count on quick success in this business; I wasn't able to support myself from my music until I was 41—until then I still had 'day jobs.' But I took great pleasure in writing and playing music all through the difficult years and never felt badly about it."[12]

Ellen Zwilich

(1939–)

In a 1990 *Peanuts* comic strip by the late Charles Schulz, Peppermint Patty and her friend Marcie are at an orchestra concert. Marcie reads the program and says, "The next piece is a concerto for flute and orchestra. It was composed by Ellen Zwilich who, incidentally, just happens to be a woman." Peppermint Patty jumps up in her seat and yells, "GOOD GOING, ELLEN!"[1]

Charles Schulz was a big fan of the music of Ellen Zwilich. It is with his approval that she created *Peanuts Gallery*, a six-part composition for orchestra and piano. The composition included pieces called "Lullaby for Linus," "Snoopy Does the Samba," "Lucy Freaks Out," "Peppermint Patty and

Ellen Taaffe Zwilich

Marcie Lead the Parade," and "Schroeder's Beethoven Fantasy." In 1997, at the end of the *Peanuts Gallery* premiere at Carnegie Hall, the children in the audience cheered and so did their parents. Ellen Zwilich was also very young when she began learning about music.

She was born Ellen Taaffe on April 30, 1939, in Miami, Florida, to Edward and Ruth Howard Taaffe. Her father was an airline pilot and her mother a homemaker. Neither of Ellen's parents had musical training, but they owned a piano. When she was still a young child, Ellen often made up songs on the piano. She recalled, "When I was three, I didn't say, 'I'm going to be a composer'—I just made music, and I thought that was a very natural thing to do."[2] By the time Ellen was five, she was taking piano lessons. Even at that young age, she thought, "This music isn't as good as the music I make up."[3] Ellen started to write her songs down when she was about ten years old.

Piano was not the only instrument Ellen played. She also studied violin and trumpet. She played violin in her high school orchestra and trumpet in the band. In addition to her playing, Ellen also composed pieces for the band and orchestra. After graduating from high school in 1956, she enrolled in Florida State University in Tallahassee, Florida. She earned a bachelor's degree in musical composition from Florida State in 1960 and a master's degree in 1962.

Ellen Taaffe spent a year teaching music in South Carolina before moving to New York City to try and make a living as a musician. She played here and there until she got a job as a violinist with the American Symphony Orchestra in 1967. Her seven years with the symphony were "very much a laboratory for me," said Ellen. "One of the great things about the American Symphony in those days was that we had the most amazing array of guest conductors."[4]

While playing with the American Symphony, Ellen Taaffe met Joseph Zwilich, a violinist with the Metropolitan Opera Orchestra. The couple married on June 22, 1969. Ellen Zwilich decided to continue her education and left the American Symphony Orchestra in 1972 to attend Juilliard School of Music. In 1975, she was the first woman to earn a doctorate in musical composition from Juilliard. Like most twentieth-century composers, Zwilich felt drawn to compose in a popular style called the twelve-tone system. This system is a highly intellectual, mathematical musical style that lacks much emotion. While still at Juilliard, Zwilich composed her Sonata for Violin and Piano using elements of the twelve-tone system in the work.

Zwilich then began working on her Chamber Symphony for Six Players. While she was composing the Chamber Symphony, Joseph Zwilich died suddenly in 1979. Ellen Zwilich said, "It's still very difficult for me to listen to the "Chamber

Symphony". I had begun writing it before Joe died, and when I came back to complete it, everything had changed . . . . I loved Joe very dearly, and miss him to this day, yet his death taught me nothing so much as the joy of being alive."[5]

The Chamber Symphony, which premiered in 1979, was an immediate success with the audience, orchestra, and conductor. The symphony seemed to express more emotion than Zwilich's previous works. She said, "It wasn't a conscious decision at all to change, but there *was* a change. I think anyone who has been through a profound personal loss finds that the world looks very different afterwards."[6]

Ellen Zwilich continued to compose for the next few years, gaining greater and greater public acceptance. She finally "arrived" as a composer with her Symphony No. 1: Three Movements for Orchestra. It premiered on May 5, 1982, and in 1983, Ellen Zwilich became the first woman ever awarded a Pulitzer Prize in music. After winning the prize, Zwilich said, "When I won the Pulitzer Prize, I was thrilled, of course, but I was surprised at the hullabaloo. People kept asking me 'how does it feel to be the first woman to win a Pulitzer Prize in music?'" She told them, "I hope it's the last time gender is more important than creativity."[7]

After Zwilich's success with Symphony No. 1, people lined up to ask her to compose music for them. Nearly every year since 1982 has seen the completion of a major work by Ellen Zwilich. Unlike many composers, she works on only one piece at a time. She tries to take a month or two off occasionally because she says composition is "an intense process, and every once in a while a composer has to get away."[8] The one area of musical composition she has avoided is opera. Zwilich explained, "I turned down the opera commission, because I realized that in one lifetime you can only get so much experience, and only go in so many different directions."[9]

In 1995, Ellen Zwilich was the first person chosen to occupy the Composer's Chair at Carnegie Hall, a position she held until 1999. Zwilich was involved with all of the programs in the hall and coordinated activities between the staff and musicians. During her tenure, she also took part in an educational project called "Conversations with Composers," which is a series of videotaped interviews she conducted with American composers.

In addition, she held a group of performances called "Making Music," which introduced new music to the public. Zwilich said, "I am a great believer in telling people as much as you can about a piece before it is performed—and telling them why you want to perform it. I've seen really huge halls almost filled for pre-concert lectures. Music has the potential to reach a much larger audience than it has."[10]

Zwilich said in a 1998 interview, "I really am having a wonderful time working on all this music. I feel like I've died and gone to heaven to be able to

Ellen Taaffe Zwilich (right) and Pat Appleson (left) take a break after a live interview on National Public Radio. Her interview focused on her work with *Peanuts* cartoonist, the late Charles Schulz.

write instrumental music for the best orchestras and performers of our time."[11] She added, "I look at a concert hall full of people, and some are there because they've been dragged by their partner, some because they think it's the thing they should do, and some because they want to give themselves to the music. And among all these people there's one person sitting there whose life is going to be changed by the concert. That's whom you write the music for."[12]

In 1999, Ellen Zwilich was chosen to be Musical America's Composer of the Year. During that same year, she was asked by Michigan State University to compose a symphony for its orchestra. Zwilich said, "It's wonderful to have major orchestras perform your work, but the future of music is the next generation. So there's something very exciting about having young musicians involved in the premiere of a new work."[13]

Chapter Notes

Chapter 1. John Philip Sousa

1. John Philip Sousa, *Marching Along* (Boston: Hale, Cushman, and Flint, 1941), p. 26.

2. Ibid., p. 27.

3. Ibid., p. 157.

4. Leslie Barker, "The Stars and Stripes Forever," *Dallas Morning News*, May 14, 1997, p. C 1.

5. Ibid.

6. Chris Pasles, "Boom Time For Sousa," *Los Angeles Times*, July 2, 1998, p. F 6.

7. Ibid.

8. Sousa, p. 364.

Chapter 2. Scott Joplin

1. Edward Berlin, *King of Ragtime: Scott Joplin and His Era* (New York: Oxford University Press, 1994), p. 6–7

2. Susan Curtis, *Dancing to a Black Man's Tune: A Life of Scott Joplin* (Columbia, Mo.: University of Missouri Press, 1994), p. 38.

3. Michael Walsh, "Music Reviews: Scott Joplin," *Time International*, August 3, 1992, p. 55.

4. Steve Graybow, "Joplin Hailed as Pioneer as 'Maple Leaf Rag' Turns 100," *Billboard*, June 23, 1999, p. 42.

5. Walsh, p. 55.

6. Edward Berlin, *Scott Joplin*, <http://www.scottjoplin.org/bio.html> (January 23, 2001).

7. Ann Holmes, "Treemonisha Full of Energy, Charm," *Houston Chronicle*, February 9, 1986, p. 4-Television.

8. Frances Trader in a letter to Carmen Bredeson, July 3, 1999.

9. Wayne Lee Gay, "After 100 Years, Scott Joplin's Ragtime Music Remains a Cultural Treasure," *Knight-Ridder/Tribune News Service*, June 1, 1999, p. K0767.

Chapter 3. Charles Ives

1. Henry Cowell and Sidney Cowell, *Charles Ives and His Music* (New York: Oxford University Press, 1969), p. 30.

2. "Charles Ives," *Composers Since 1900, 1981 Update*, <http://vweb.hwwilsonweb.com> (September 24, 2000).

3. Jay Feldman, "Sports Were Music to His Ears," *Sports Illustrated*, October 7, 1991, p. 106.

4. "Charles Ives," *Composers Since 1900, 1981 Update*, <http://vweb.hwwilsonweb.com> (September 24, 2000).

5. "Charles Ives," *Current Biography*, n.d. <http://vweb.hwwilsonweb.com> (September 26, 2000).

6. "Charles Ives," *Composers Since 1900, 1981 Update*, <http://vweb.hwwilsonweb.com> (September 24, 2000).

7. Terry Teachout, "The Anti-Modern Modernist," *Commentary*, May 1997, p. 55.

8. Cowell and Cowell, p. 41.

9. Teachout, p. 55.

10. Ibid., p. 55.

Chapter 4. George Gershwin

1. Edward Oxford, "George Gershwin: An American Rhapsody," *USA Today Magazine*, September 1, 1998. <http://www.elibrary.com/s/edumark> (February 7, 2001).

2. Merle, Armitage, ed., *George Gershwin: Man and Legend* (New York: Duell, Sloan and Pearce, 1938), p.11.

3. Ibid.

4. Richard Jerome, "Born 100 Years Ago, George Gershwin Set the Music World on Its Ear With Rhapsody Rhythms That Still Fascinate," *People Weekly*, November 9, 1998, p. 73.

5. Oxford, "George Gershwin: An American Rhapsody."

6. Edward Jablonski, "Gershwin Centennial Edition" (Cleveland, Ohio: TELARC International Corporation, 1998), p. 9.

7. Howard Reich, "They All Love Gershwin," *Downbeat,* September 1998, p. 18.

8. Jerome, p. 73.

9. Reich, p. 18.

Chapter 5. Duke Ellington

1. Duke Ellington, *Music Is My Mistress* (Garden City, N.Y.: Doubleday & Co., 1973), p. 20.

2. "Duke Ellington," *Current Biography,* <http://vwebhwwilsonweb.com> (October 15, 2000).

3. Ellington, p. 9.

4. Ibid.

5. Sharon Fitzgerald, "To Love Him Madly," *American Visions,* April 1999, p. 16.

6. John Edward Hasse, *Beyond Category: The Life and Genius of Duke Ellington* (New York: De Capo Press, 1993), p. 378.

7. *Duke Ellington's Sacred Concerts,* Image VHS (Chatsworth, Calif.: Image Entertainment, 1998).

8. Hasse, pp. 375–378.

9. Patricia Spears Jones, "The Immortal Duke Ellington," *Essence,* May 1999, p. 218.

10. Thor Christensen, "Duke Ellington: A Man For All Music," *Knight-Rider/Tribune News Service,* April 23, 1999, p. 1C.

Chapter 6. Aaron Copland

1. Michael Walsh, "It Sounded So Glorius to Me," *Time,* December 17, 1990, p. 113.

2. "Aaron Copland," *Composers Since 1900, 1981 Update,* <http://vweb.hwwilsonweb.com> (September 24, 2000).

3. Howard Pollack, *Aaron Copland: The Life and Work of An Uncommon Man* (New York: Henry Holt & Co., 1999), p. 223.

4. Ibid., p. 323.

5. Kenneth La Fave, "Celebrating Copland's America," *The Arizona Republic*, September 17, 2000, p. E1.

6. Robert Bagar and Louis Biancolli, *Concert Companion* (New York: McGraw-Hill, 1947), p. 189.

7. Ibid., p. 190.

8. "Aaron Copland," *Composers Since 1900, 1981 Update*, <http://vwweb.hwwilssonweb.com> (September 24, 2000).

9. Charles Ward, "Copland, the American Master," *Houston Chronicle*, October 1, 2000, p. 10 Zest.

10. La Fave, p. E1.

Chapter 7. Samuel Barber

1. "Samuel Barber," *Composers Since 1900, 1981 Update*, <http://vweb.hwwilsonweb.com> (September 24, 2000).

2. Terry Teachout, "Samuel Barber's Revenge," *Commentary*, April 1996, p. 55.

3. Ibid.

4. Ibid.

5. Barbara Heyman, *Samuel Barber: The Composer and His Music* (New York: Oxford University Press, 1992), p. 173.

6. "Samuel Barber," *Composers Since 1900, 1981 Update*, <http://vweb.hwwilsonweb.com> (September 24, 2000).

7. Ralph Thibodeau, "Softness, Intensity Highlight Horowitz Comeback Concert," *Corpus Christi Caller Times*, April 1, 1975, p. B4.

8. "Samuel Barber," *Composers Since 1900, 1981 Update*, <http://vweb.hwwilsonweb.com> (September 24, 2000).

9. Ibid.

Chapter 8. Leonard Bernstein

1. "Leonard Bernstein," *Musicians Since 1900*, <http://vweb.hwwilsonweb.com> (May 25, 2000).

2. Daniel Webster, "Leonard Bernstein," *Knight-Ridder/Tribune News Service*, May 25, 1994 0525K4249.

3. "Leonard Bernstein," *Musicians Since 1900*, <http://vweb.hwwilsonweb.com> (May 25, 2000).

4. Ibid.

5. Jamie Bernstein Thomas, "The Media Maestro," *Newsweek*, June 28, 1999, p. 56.

6. Joan Peyser, *Bernstein: A Biography* (New York: Billboard Books, 1998), p. 186.

7. Ralph Thibodeau, "The Media Is the Mass," *Commonweal*, October 1, 1971, p. 17.

8. Thomas, p. 56.

9. Schuyler Chapin, "Leonard Bernstein, RIP," *National Review*, November 19, 1990, p. 19.

10. "Leonard Bernstein," *Life*, Fall 1990, p. 10.

Chapter 9. Philip Glass

1. "Philip Glass," *Current Biography and World Musicians*, <http://vweb.hwwilsonweb.com> (September 24, 2000).

2. "Philip Glass," *Composers Since 1900*, <http://vweb.hwwilsonweb.com> (September 24, 2000).

3. Michael Walsh, "Music: Making a Joyful Noise," *Time*, June 3, 1985, p. 72.

4. "Philip Glass," *Composers Since 1900*, <http://vweb.hwwilsonweb.com> (September 24, 2000).

5. Walsh, p. 73.

6. Richard Kostelanetz, ed., *Writings on Glass: Essays, Interviews, and Criticism* (Los Angeles: University of California Press, 1997), p. 172.

7. Ibid., p. 243.

8. Walsh, p. 73.

9. Ibid.

10. Peter Goddard, "Philip Glass Meets Dracula," *The Toronto Star*, November 6, 2000. <http://www.elibrary.com> (January 21, 2001).

11. Kerry Lengel, "Humble Composer Settling a Score," *The Arizona Republic*, October 15, 2000, p. E3.

12. Kostelanetz, p. 278.

Chapter 10. Ellen Zwilich

1. Tim Smith, "Composer By the Sea," *Sun-Sentinel*, April 3, 1994, p. D.1.

2. "Ellen Zwilich," *Current Biography and World Musicians, 1998 Update,* <http://vweb.hwwilsonweb.com> (September 24, 2000).

3. Katrine Ames, "The Kids in the Hall," *Newsweek*, April 21, 1997, p. 78.

4. Janelle Gelfand, "Performance Background Is Evident in Zwilich's Compositions," *Gannett News Service,* October 8, 2000, p. ARC.

5. "Ellen Zwilich," *Current Biography and World Musicians, 1998 Update,* <http://vweb.hwwilsonweb.com> (September 24, 2000).

6. Smith, p. D1.

7. Charles Paikert, "Composed Composer," *US*, May 7, 1984, p. 62.

8. Heidi Waleson, "Composer Ellen Taaffe Zwilich: Living Her Dream," *Symphony Magazine*, April/May 1986.

9. Ibid.

10. Smith, p. D1.

11. K. Robert Schwarz, "A Composer Who Actually Earns a Living Composing," *The New York Times*, March 22, 1998, p. 38.

12. Ibid.

13. John Schaefer, "Composer Ellen Taaffe Zwilich," *Musical America: International Directory of the Performing Arts*, p. 28.

Further Reading

Books

Brown, Gene. *Duke Ellington: Jazz Master.* Woodbridge, CT: Blackbirch Press, 2001.

Copland, Aaron. *Copland. Since 1943.* New York: St. Martin's Press, 1990.

Lazo, Caroline Evensen. *Leonard Bernstein: In Love with Music.* Minneapolis: Lerner, 2003.

Nichols, Janet. *American Music Makers: An Introduction to American Composers.* New York: Walker and Co., 1990.

Old, Wendie. *Duke Ellington: Giant of Jazz.* Springfield, N.J.: Enslow Publishers, 1996.

Reef, Catherine. *George Gershwin: American Composer.* Greensboro, N.C.: Morgan Reynolds Inc., 2000.

Sabir, C. Ogbu. *Scott Joplin: The King of Ragtime.* Chanhassen, MN: Child's World, 2001.

Sive, Helen R. *Music's Connecticut Yankee: An Introduction to the Life and Music of Charles Ives.* New York: Atheneum, 1977.

Zannos, Susan. *The Life and Times of John Philip Sousa.* Hockessin, Del.: Mitchell Lane Publishers, 2004.

Videos

An American in Paris. Santa Monica, Calif.: MGM Home Entertainment, 1998. (Music by George Gershwin)

Leonard Bernstein's Young People's Concerts with the New York Philharmonic. New York: Sony Classical, 1993.

Rhapsody in Blue: The Story of George Gershwin. Culver City, Calif.: Warner Brothers Pictures, Inc., 1991.

Stars and Stripes Forever. Los Angeles, Calif.: Fox Video, 1991. (Music of John Philip Sousa)

Internet Addresses

John Philip Sousa: American Composer, Conductor and Patriot.
<http://www.dws.org/sousa/index.htm>

Scott Joplin International Ragtime Foundation located in Sedalia, Missouri.
<http://www.scottjoplin.org/>

Charles Ives Biography.
<http://www.schirmer.com/composers/ives_bio.html>

George Gershwin: A Tribute to America's Greatest Composer.
<http://www.ffaire.com/gershwin/>

Duke Ellington: Celebrating 100 Years of the Man and His Music.
<http://www.dellington.org/>

The **Aaron Copland** Collection, Library of Congress.
<http://memory.loc.gov/ammem/achtml/achome.html>

Samuel Barber: I Hear America Singing.
<http://www.wnet.org/ihas/composer/barber.html>

The **Leonard Bernstein** Collection, Library of Congress.
<http://memory.loc.gov/ammem/lbhtml/lbhome.html>

The Official Web Site of **Philip Glass**.
<http://www.philipglass.com/>

Ellen Taffe Zwilich, Biography and Works.
<http://www.presser.com/composers/zwilich.html>

Index

About the Authors

Ralph Thibodeau and Carmen Thibodeau Bredeson are the father and daughter authors of *Ten Great American Composers.*

Carmen Bredeson is the author of thirty nonfiction books for young people. She is a former high school English teacher and has a master's degree in instructional technology. In addition to fund-raising and performing volunteer work for public libraries, Bredeson now devotes much of her time to writing. Her recent Enslow books include *Mount St. Helens Volcano* and *NASA Planetary Spacecraft.*

Ralph Thibodeau is a professor emeritus of music history, music literature, and western humanities for Del Mar College, Corpus Christi, Texas, where he taught for thirty years. He was also a music critic for the *Corpus Christi Caller-Times* newspaper for twenty years. Prior to his teaching career, Ralph Thibodeau served as a Navy pilot and landing signal officer in the Atlantic Fleet during World War II.

9/06,0